| DATE | | | |
|---|---|---|---|
| | | | |
| | | | |
| | | | |
| | | | |
| | | | |
| | | | |
| | | | |
| | | | |
| | | | |
| | | | |
| | | | |
| | | | |

BY LARRY DANE BRIMNER

# MOUNTAIN BIKING

## A FIRST BOOK

**FRANKLIN WATTS**
A Division of Grolier Publishing
New York   London   Hong Kong   Sydney
Danbury, Connecticut

Readers should remember that all sports carry a certain amount of risk. To reduce that risk while mountain biking, ride at your own level, wear all safety equipment, and use care and common sense. The author and publisher will take no responsibility or liability for injuries resulting from the use of mountain bikes.

Photographs ©: Outside Images: cover, 30, 50, 54 (Bob Allen), 5, 20, 24, 36 (Steve Behr), 22, 41 (Doug Berry), 7, 11, 14, 26, 29, 32, 35, 44, 48, 53 (Jamie Bloomquist), 12 (Skip Brown), 40 (Darcy Kiefel), 42, 46, 57, 58 (Bill Thomas), 2 (T. R. Youngstrom).

Brimner, Larry Dane.
    Mountain biking / by Larry Dane Brimner.
      p.   cm. — (a first book)
    Includes bibliographical references and index.
    Summary: Describes the history, equipment, safety tips, and competitive riding of mountain bikes.
    ISBN 0-531-20243-7(lib.bdg.)    ISBN 0-531-15814-4 (pbk.)
    1. All terrain cycling—juvenile literature. [1. All terrain cycling.]
I. Title. II. Series.
GV1056.B75 1996
796.6—dc20                        96-6413
                                         CIP
                                         AC

# CONTENTS

*For the kids at Bayfield Elementary,*
*Bayfield, Colorado*

*Mountain bikes must be built to withstand
the jarring action of "bunny hops."*

# IN THE
# BEGINNING

Mountain biking has its roots in the beginnings of bicycle history. Around 1869, the first pedal-powered *velocipede* appeared on American streets. Arriving from Europe, it had wooden wheels, steel rims with no tires, and a rigid frame. Appropriately enough, it was called a "boneshaker." It required a full revolution of the pedals to achieve a full revolution of the front wheel. Stopping was achieved by a novel device: the rider's feet—dragging them provided the machine's only breaking mechanism.

In the mid-1870s, a bicycle called the "ordinary" was developed. Although top-heavy and unstable, it allowed the rider to cover more ground per pedal rotation. But it was also difficult to mount. The rider was seated over a front wheel that measured 5 feet in diameter!

By 1890, the "safety," a low, chain-driven bicycle began to appear. With smaller wheels and sprockets mounted front and rear, the safety allowed each rotation of the pedals to produce added distance. With the introduction of air-inflated tires at about the same time, bicycles acquired a cushioned ride, and interest in riding them spread hither and yon. Bicycles replaced the horse and buggy as a common mode of transportation. They were even used as military vehicles. The U.S. Army's Twenty-fifth Bicycle Corps Regiment was prepared to defend the country on two wheels. The boom might have lasted had it not been for the mass production of automobiles. Gasoline-powered automobiles captured the interest of adults, and bicycling was given up to children.

In the 1960s, however, a new bike boom began. The invention of a multisprocket speed-changing mechanism called a *derailleur*, a French word meaning "gearshift," meant that riders could tackle just about any terrain with relative ease. With its introduction, many grown-ups returned to two-wheeled transportation.

Bicycles of the 1960s, though, had skinny tires. Put one of these bikes on rugged terrain or in loose sand or dirt, and the riders may as well have been on foot. The skinny-tired bikes simply had no traction.

Yet riders often wanted to venture off the beaten tracks with their bikes. Enter the BMX bicycle. The initials stand for bicycle motocross, as riders were duplicating many of the stunts and events popular with riders of gasoline-powered dirt bikes in motorcycle motocross, or MX. BMX bicycles were low slung, small wheeled, and fat tired, and they were built to withstand the punishment of rough,

*Uniquely American, mountain bikes were built*
*to venture off the beaten path.*

*In West Virginia, a family takes an outing on their mountain bikes.*

hard riding. But they were unsuited to long-distance hill climbing because they typically had only one speed.

Interested in backcountry hill climbing, a group of people from northern California began tinkering with an assortment of bicycles. Scavenging parts, they added sprockets so the bikes would have multiple speeds to ascend and descend slopes. They replaced stock frames with newer, more durable, lighter-weight materials. And soon they were venturing where before only mules and jeeps could go.

Today, mountain bikes and the riders commanding them can be found exploring everything from New York City streets to Sierra Nevada trails. Best of all, the machines are bringing families together, as mountain biking is as popular with young people as it is with grown-ups.

*A boulder is a worthy challenge
for this mountain-bike rider.*

# THE
# BIKEſ

A mountain bike differs from most other bikes in that it is designed to provide a stable ride while bumping along rough dirt trails. At its heart is a rugged frame. Most mountain-bike frames are made of light weight chrome-moly steel, aluminum, titanium, or a composite (combination of any two materials). These bikes weigh from 20 to 28 pounds (9–13 kg), compared with the 90-pound (41 kg) monsters used by the U.S. Army's Twenty-fifth Bicycle Corps Regiment.

The frame of a mountain bike differs from that of a regular touring bike in a couple of other ways. The first is that the tubing used in frame construction is usually slightly larger in diameter. This provides added strength. The second difference is that a mountain-bike frame is usually lower and stretched out for a longer wheelbase (the distance between the front-wheel axle and the rear-wheel axle). This lowers the center of gravity, which means that a mountain-bike rider has greater stability and control.

Wheels are the next most important feature of a mountain bike. Unlike the wheels of touring bikes, those of a mountain bike are smaller in diameter. Again, this helps to lower the center of gravity, putting the rider closer to the riding surface for better stability and control. Most mountain-bike wheels are aluminum rimmed, which allows brake pads to grip better than steel rims in wet weather.

Because mountain bikes are meant to traverse all kinds of terrain, they usually have tires with a larger tread width than those on touring bikes. The larger tires allow for a bigger footprint; in other words, more tire comes into contact with the riding surface, and this provides better traction. A knobby tread pattern also improves traction because the knobs help grip loose terrain. Anyone who has ever tried to ride a skinny-wheeled touring bike through sand or loose dirt will understand the benefits of balloon tires. Skinny-wheeled bikes sink into a soft surface and go nowhere, while bikes with fat tires maintain mobility.

On the other hand, fat tires slow riders down on smooth, hard surfaces because they create added friction. For this reason, some mountain-bike riders who race on courses with varying surfaces choose tires with slightly smaller tread widths. In deciding which tire will suit your needs, you need to consider the kind of riding that you will be doing. Fatter tires (26 x 2.125 in.) are superior on the loose surfaces that you'll likely encounter in the backcountry. Narrower tires (26 x 1.75 in.) will do just fine if your riding is confined to city streets. A good, dual-purpose tire is 26 x 2 inches; it is wide enough to provide traction on loose dirt, while narrow enough to allow speed on hard surfaces. In the end, it comes down to a rider's personal preference. Experience, experimentation, and talking with other mountain bikers will help you decide.

Most casual mountain bikers don't need to concern themselves with a bicycle's drivetrain. The drivetrain consists of the crank set, the rear sprocket cluster, and the chain. These produce a bicycle's forward movement when a rider pushes on the pedals. The crank set itself is usually made up of three different-sized sprockets, or chain rings, each having a different number of teeth. For most riders, the stock crank set provided by your bicycle's manufacturer will be sufficient. Some serious mountain bikers, however, customize their crank sets. They replace the stock crank sets with others that have sprockets with more or fewer teeth to create the variety of gears that they want. There are many varieties to choose from to fit an individual's riding needs.

The rear sprocket cluster may have as many as seven toothed cogs of different sizes. The number of gears a bicycle has is determined by multiplying the number of front chain rings by the number of cogs at the rear. A bicycle with a three-ring crank set and a rear sprocket cluster having seven cogs, gives you twenty-one speeds, or gears, to choose from.

You shift gears by engaging the front and rear derailleurs. Unlike many touring bikes, the shifters on mountain bikes are mounted to the handlebars so that the rider may operate them with the thumbs and index fingers.

# ANATOMY OF A MOUNTAIN BIKE

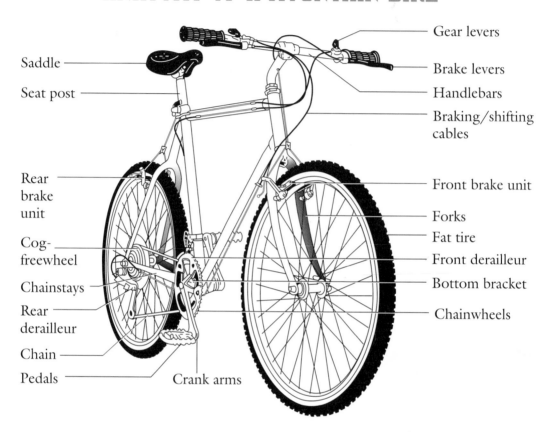

Gear levers

Saddle

Brake levers

Seat post

Handlebars

Braking/shifting cables

Rear brake unit

Front brake unit

Cog-freewheel

Forks

Fat tire

Chainstays

Front derailleur

Rear derailleur

Bottom bracket

Chain

Chainwheels

Pedals

Crank arms

The advantage of this is that you can shift gears and still keep a firm grip on the handlebars. This is an important control feature when you're jostling along switchback trails.

The unique shape of a mountain bike's handlebars is another control feature, and one that makes a mountain bike easily recognizable from touring bikes. Rather than the dropped bars of touring bikes, mountain bikes have flat bars. These enable you to sit more upright, putting you in a better position to see the trail ahead.

Another control concern that all mountain bikers share is the ability to slow down and stop. Almost all mountain bikes use cantilever brakes that, when engaged, stop by means of the friction caused when the brake pads grip the wheel rim.

Two other components round out the mountain bike. The seat, or saddle, is generally wider and softer than those found on touring bikes. And the pedals tend to have toothed edges to grip the rider's shoes, rather than straps or clips. Because mountain bikers often must use their feet to take a curve or to prevent a spill, they must be able to move their feet quickly. The straps or clips common to touring bikes impede quick movement and pose a safety threat to the mountain-bike rider.

Just like automobiles, mountain bikes are available with accessories. One recent trend is to equip bikes with special shock-absorbing suspension systems and handlebar stems that guarantee a smoother, more comfortable ride. These are nice extras, but they also add to the cost of the bike. If you are a casual mountain biker, you can have just as much fun without the fancy equipment. A basic mountain bike will still take you anywhere, anytime.

*Imagine attempting this on
a skinny-wheeled touring bike!*

# CHOOSING THE RIGHT BIKE

Mountain bikes are meant to be ridden in the harshest of environments, so you'll want one that is built to withstand punishment. It's best to shop around before you buy. Bike and sporting-goods shops are good places to see what's available and to strike up conversations with personnel who are experienced mountain-bike riders. Don't be afraid to ask questions. Find out what brand the salesperson rides. Ask what he or she likes about it, and what its disadvantages are.

Mountain bikes are not an inexpensive investment, and the adage "you get what you pay for" has some merit. You can pay anywhere from a few hundred dollars for a good mountain bike to several thousand for top quality.

It's a good idea to keep in mind the kind of riding that you plan on doing before you under- or overinvest. Most

*Knobby tires provide traction on smooth rock surfaces.*

riders don't need to spend thousands of dollars on a quality mountain bike because riding usually will be limited to "weekend warrior" routines and more casual neighborhood outings. If, however, you plan on serious competition or extensive off-road trekking, a bigger investment might be wise. If you simply don't know at this point whether or not you'll take to mountain biking, get some experience on a *good* mountain bike before moving up to *quality*. The fact is that the majority of riding that mountain bikers do is on pavement, not rugged terrain, so a good mountain bike costing in the range of a few hundred dollars will satisfy the needs of most riders.

It is important to get the right measure when choosing a mountain bike. To do this, stand flat-footed astride the frame. Because mountain bikes are meant to have a lower center of gravity, there should be 2 to 4 inches of clearance between you and the top tube. The size of a bike is measured by the distance between the middle of the bottom bracket and the top of the seat tube. Most mountain bikes range between 17 and 23 inches. Personal adjustments are made by raising or lowering the saddle and handlebars.

*This bicycle courier must stay alert in London's busy traffic.*

# PREPARING TO RIDE

Mountain bikes are built to withstand punishment. Riders are not. No matter how rugged you think you are, you risk injury if you are not properly prepared for a ride.

Whatever else you decide to wear, *always* put on a helmet to protect yourself against head injuries. A good helmet meets the standards of the American National Standards Institute and displays the institution's name or ANSI acronym on the helmet label. Helmets that display the green, blue, or white Snell Memorial Foundation sticker meet even more rigid standards.

Helmets are made of a hard, impact-resistant outer shell and a polystyrene foam inner liner. The fit should be snug, but not uncomfortable. The chin strap should be adjustable and allow for quick release. Bicycle helmets are

*This rider is using her head. You should **NEVER** mount your bike without a good helmet.*

lightweight and have air vents to allow hot air to escape and cool air to enter. As a result, they are comfortable to wear.

Today's bicycle helmets come in a variety of styles and colors. The choice is yours. Some have sun visors built into them. Others are streamlined to cut down on wind resistance, an important concern to racers. Apart from the bicycle itself, a helmet is a mountain biker's most basic piece of equipment. *Use your head; never pedal without a helmet securely in place.* In fact, you may be breaking the law if you ride without one!

Anything else a mountain biker wears is up to personal taste, the weather, and the riding environment. Many riders prefer regular street clothes; others like to outfit themselves with clothing designed specifically for biking. Before choosing your riding clothes, however, consider these points:

- Loose clothing tends to catch the air, slowing down rider and machine.

- Baggy clothing runs the risk of getting caught in the machinery—the chain, sprockets, and spokes.

- Tight clothing that doesn't allow freedom of movement is uncomfortable.

For these reasons, many riders choose riding clothes made of a blend of nylon and Lycra®. This stretchy, synthetic material follows the contours of the body, cutting wind resistance to a minimum. It also allows the rider complete freedom of movement. Pants—available in mid-thigh length, knee length, and ankle length—often come with extra padding in the crotch area or inserts for comfort and to prevent chafing.

Jerseys come with short or long sleeves. Many have pockets across the lower back for small essentials.

In cold weather, layer your clothes. Several layers of lightweight clothing will provide better insulation than one heavy layer. Plus, layers allow the rider the option of taking off an outer garment if the day turns warm.

Riding gloves are a nice accessory. The palms are padded for comfort, so gloves help to absorb the jolts that travel up through the handlebars. Be sure your gloves are snug when purchased because they will stretch with use.

Whether you ride on urban and suburban streets or on trails in the brush, eye protection is essential. A pair of sunglasses that screens ultraviolet light will not only protect your eyes from the sun's harmful rays, but also from the dust and particles kicked up when riding. Some cycling glasses have interchangeable clear lenses for use on overcast days or when you ride at night.

Most weekend mountain bikers can get by with a pair of good cross-training shoes or lightweight hiking boots. Just be sure the soles of the shoes are firm and grip the pedals. Pay special attention to the laces. Long laces should be tucked inside the shoe. If they flap about in the breeze, they may become entwined around the crank and pose a hazard.

Special mountain-biking shoes are available, and they often have a strap to secure laces out of the way. They also have a deep tread for gripping the toothed edges of the pedals, as well as for providing traction when walking on loose terrain. Traditionally, mountain bikers have shied away from the cleated and clipless shoes popular with road

*Cold weather need not deter your riding*
*if you wear suitable clothing.*

*A long distance rider, packing his gear,
is off on a peaceful adventure.*

racers because they restricted feet movement. Newer designs, however, have been adapted specifically for mountain bikes. For the serious mountain biker, these specialized shoes can link rider and bike for maximum power output, but they take getting used to.

Long-distance biking requires planning ahead. If you plan to sleep out under the stars, you'll want to carry a lightweight tent and sleeping bag. Water and food should also be high on your list of things to take with you. Obviously, the disadvantage to long-distance biking is packing all the extra equipment and weight. Many long-distance bikers avoid this by planning each day's journey so that they can stay overnight at a hotel and eat in restaurants. This requires a little extra planning, but the trade-off may be worth it if you dislike maneuvering the extra 20 to 30 pounds (9–14 kg) of equipment.

You should also carry a few basic tools with you on any long ride. A typical tool kit includes a screwdriver, bicycle-tire irons, a pair of pliers, an adjustable wrench, Allen wrenches, and a tire-patching kit. As cumbersome as this all sounds, breakdowns usually occur at the most inconvenient times, and it pays to be prepared. To be otherwise is to be setting yourself up for a long hike home.

*When bicycle lanes are provided, use them.*

# ON CITY
# STREETS

Although mountain bikes are built for rugged, off-road terrain, most riders use them on city streets. Their design makes them suitable for any terrain or environment. When used in urban settings, however, they are called city bikes by dedicated off-road enthusiasts. This not-so-subtle insult suggests that urban riding lacks the challenges of *real* mountain biking. This may be true to a certain extent, but riding on city streets presents its own unique challenges.

The greatest of these challenges is sharing the road with automobiles. If you plan to bicycle side-by-side automobiles, be smart. *Always wear your helmet*. Head injuries are a cyclist's greatest fear and the most common serious bicycle injury. Also, stay alert. The best way to stay out of harm's way is to avoid hazards. Just as if you were driving an automobile, look ahead to anticipate potential difficulties. Is there a loose dog? Are you approaching a pothole or drainage grate? Might somebody in a parked car swing open a door? These are potentially dangerous situations that an alert cyclist will spot—and avoid.

A bicyclist must abide by the same laws that govern automobile traffic. Ride with the flow of traffic. A bicycle moving in the opposite direction may go unnoticed by drivers merging into traffic. Obey stop signs and signal lights. Stay to the right, unless you are preparing to turn left. Left turns should usually be made from the lane farthest left in the direction of travel. If there is heavy traffic, however, dismount and walk your bike across at a pedestrian crosswalk.

Because biking has become so popular, more and more communities are setting aside dedicated bicycle lanes. Use them when they are present. Automobile drivers are supposed to respect the purpose of these lanes and stay out of them. Some drivers, however, don't. Be aware of this; and if a car should drift into your bicycle lane, take evasive action rather than playing the game of chicken. A car represents a couple of *tons* of fox to your mountain bike's 20 to 28 *pounds* (9-13 kg) of chicken!

Weaving and swerving in and out of traffic is not only inconsiderate of others using a roadway, but it is also dangerous. Be a considerate rider. Ride in a straight path, single file if you are riding with others. Stunts should be reserved for areas that are free of traffic and other hazards.

How many saddles does a mountain bike have? Unless it is a bicycle designed for tandem riding, it will have only one saddle. This means there should be only one rider. Don't carry passengers, as it throws the bicycle out of bal-

*Always obey posted signs.*

ance. An out-of-balance bicycle is difficult to control. Neither should you hitch a ride by holding onto moving vehicles. Some riders think that this stunt is both daring and energy conserving. It isn't. It's stupid!

Cycling on city streets can be as challenging and rewarding as off-road riding. You will observe more details than people passing in automobiles, and you will move more swiftly than pedestrians. (In some instances, you will move more swiftly than automobiles!) At the same time, you will be benefiting your overall health and well-being. The key to happy cycling on city streets is to respect the big guy, the automobile, and to be alert.

*A trio of riders sets off into the backcountry.*

# INTO THE
# BACKCOUNTRY

Although urban riding can be invigorating, nothing beats the rugged backcountry for the sense of exploration, quality of fresh air, and challenge of meeting nature on its own terms. It's a great way to share time with friends, but the solitude of solo riding can also be satisfying. Your mountain bike, with its chubby tires and sturdy construction, can take you places that you would never dare to venture on a skinny-wheeled racing bike.

Whenever setting out for the backcountry, at least carry water and a few light snacks. And unless you're exploring an area where the weather is fairly predictable, it's a good idea to stuff a windbreaker into your backpack. As with urban riding, *always wear your helmet.* Spills are not uncommon when riding on rough terrain, so give yourself as much protection as possible.

When tackling trails in the backcountry, you'll call upon specific riding skills that you ordinarily don't need in the city. The most important of these is an understanding of the gears.

Your mountain bike most likely has a chainwheel assembly made up of three chain rings, or sprockets, attached to the right crank. At the rear are six or seven free-wheel cogs, which are also called sprockets. Ideally, you want to position the chain on the front and rear sprockets to produce resistance when you pedal, but not so much resistance that your legs are overworked. For most riding, the middle chain ring (on the front sprocket) will be the one used. Pair this with a rear sprocket that produces a comfortable resistance level. For high-speed riding or when descending a steep hill, you'll shift the chain to the large chain ring in the front sprocket and to a freewheel cog that produces the right amount of resistance. The small chain ring is used for uphill climbing. By shifting the chain to the largest freewheel cog at the rear, you'll be able to tackle almost any incline.

Experience will teach you which gears are best for the terrain you're tackling and your own physical strength. But there are a couple of rules of thumb to follow. The first is that the largest chain ring (front sprocket) should not be used in conjunction with the largest freewheel cog (rear sprocket), or conversely, the smallest chain ring with the smallest freewheel cog. Such combinations stress the chain and cause excessive wear on the sprockets. The second thing to remember is to keep your weight over the rear wheel when climbing a hill, as it helps to maintain traction.

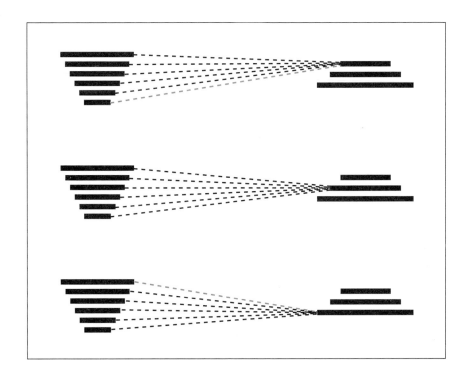

Once a mountain has been climbed, you need to get back down. The secret to a safe descent is control. Never ride beyond your abilities. Always stay in control of your bike. If you have doubts about your ability to descend a slope safely, dismount and walk it down. There is nothing embarrassing about pushing your bike downhill, or uphill. At times, there is no other way, and even the most experienced riders succumb to this time-proven technique.

Brakes are essential to a safe and sane descent. But never apply your front brake first. If you do, you may dive right over the handlebars. Instead, rely on the rear brake, using the front brake sparingly to maintain control.

When descending, your body posture will be different than it is when ascending or riding on level pavement. Keep the pedals horizontal. Stay low, and slide yourself back off the seat. The steeper the descent, the farther back and more stretched out you want to be.

*When descending a hill, slide yourself back off the seat.*

*Especially steep terrain may require riding out of the saddle.*

With mastery of these few basic techniques, you will be ready for whatever terrain may greet you. More ad-vanced maneuvering techniques—like varying the tire pressure, standing out of the saddle, tucking for speed, and "hopsta-cles"—will be gained through experience, further reading, and observation of and discussion with more advanced riders.

*Observed Trials riding is precision riding.*

# COMPETITIVE RIDING

If you're itching to test your riding skill and see how it compares with the skills of other riders, then you'll want to compete. Mountain-bike competitions come in many forms and varieties, from slow to fast and from mild to wild. Something is certain to appeal to you. Most mountain-bike competitions are governed by the National Off-Road Bicycle Association (NORBA), but you need not wait for a NORBA event to practice your skills. There's no reason why you and your friends can't chart out a course yourselves and compete against each other.

*In trials competition, be prepared for any obstacle.*

# OBSERVED TRIALS

One competitive event that will really test your riding skills is the Observed Trials course, which was derived from a motorcycle competition. This event is sometimes called Trialsin, because its object is to complete the course with as few errors, or sins, as possible.

Each Trials course is divided into segments, or sections, of difficult terrain that is littered with obstacles, including boulders, logs, mud, sand, and anything else a fiendish mind can think of. Usually, a course will have ten sections; the rider's goal is to complete each section without dabbing a foot to the ground, tumbling, straying out of bounds, or stopping. A monitor, or checker, records faults on a scorecard as the rider negotiates each section. A perfect score of zero is the desired outcome, but it's easier said than done.

Observed Trials is not a speed event, nor is it a test of endurance. Rather, it is a test of precision riding and balance. To win in this event, you need to be a master of your machine.

# RACING

If adrenaline, speed, and risk are what make you function, then one of the mountain-bike racing events is sure to catch your eye. These events are about reading the terrain, taking corners, and getting from start to finish lickety-split.

*A rider competes against the clock in downhill racing.*

Downhill racing is the grandfather of mountain-bike racing events. In it, one racer at a time tries to descend a dirt track as a clock ticks away the time. As in downhill skiing, the rider who completes the course in the shortest amount of time wins the event.

Cross-country racing is about both speed and endurance. The 5- to 15-mile (8–24 km) courses may involve steep climbs and descents, but most of it will be run on dirt roads and trails wide enough for passing safely. The key to successful cross-country competition is to focus on finishing. Compete against yourself and not against other riders when you first begin flirting with this event. Use your first few races to determine which skills you need to strengthen. Work on those. Then start entering to win.

One competitive event that is suited to an urban or suburban park setting is the short-course race. Measuring up to a few miles or kilometers, a short-course race might include paved roads, grassy lawns, and a shot through a muddy trail.

Once again borrowing from the sport of skiing, the dual slalom is an event in which two riders descend identical side-by-side courses at the same time. The rider getting to the bottom of the hill first, without missing any of the gates, wins the race.

Hill climbs are a popular racing event, one borrowed from motorcycle competition. In one kind of hill climb, the rider who gets to the top of the hill first wins. In the other kind, the site is purposely chosen because the hill cannot be conquered. In this instance, the rider who goes the farthest up the hill will take home the prize.

# BICYCLE POLO

Although not a racing event, the sport of bicycle polo has become quite popular. The rules are similar to those used for equine polo, and the game is played on a polo lawn. The obvious advantage of bicycle polo is that there are no huge feed bills for your mount.

*Polo teams now form leagues and compete against each other.*

Whether you choose to sign up for organized events or face off against a few friends, mountain-bike competitions will test your riding abilities and give you a heart-thumping experience in the process. Best of all, you'll be surrounded by other mountain-bike enthusiasts who share your enthusiasm.

## HOT RIDES

Chequamegon Fat Tire Festival (Wisconsin)
Fat Tire Week (Crested Butte, Colorado)
Iditabike (Alaska)
Iron Horse Classic (Colorado)
Mammoth Mountain Kamikaze (California)
Moab Mountain Bike Festival (Utah)
Mt. Snow Race (Vermont)
Revenge of the Siskiyous (Oregon)
West Virginia Fat Tire Festival (West Virginia)
Whistler Mountain (British Columbia, Canada)

Although mountain bikes are American in origin, their popularity has spread worldwide. For information about mountain biking in countries other than the United States and Canada, contact the tourist board of the country you're interested in or one of the tour companies listed in Chapter 10. Publications at your local bike shop are another good source. For information about one of the ten Hot Rides, contact NORBA.

*Go-anywhere machines need routine inspections
to stand up to this type of riding.*

# KEEPING YOUR BIKE FIT

Although a mountain bike is ruggedly built, it will need regular maintenance to keep it in trail-worthy condition. Keeping an eye out for problems as they develop will help avoid major disasters when you're 50 miles (80 km) from the nearest services.

A bike that is ridden often under extremely harsh conditions needs tuning more often than one that is ridden seasonally under moderate conditions. Whether you do the work yourself or have somebody else do it, a mountain bike, to remain fit and ready for travel, should be tuned yearly or twice-yearly and inspected on a weekly basis.

A weekly inspection includes a check to make sure that the tires are properly inflated. Repair or replace the tubes if necessary. If you are prone to picking up thorns and nails in your tires, it might be a good idea to install a flat-proof tube. Although this type of tube is not really flat-proof, it is designed with a slightly thicker outer perimeter so that it is less susceptible to punctures than regular tubes.

Check the handbrakes. When the brake pads are in full contact with the wheel rims, there should be a gap between the handbrake levers and the handlebars. If the handbrake levers come into contact with the handlebars, adjust the cables according to the manufacturer's directions.

At the same time you check the handbrakes, inspect the brake blocks, or pads. If they have become off kilter, adjust them with a wrench and Allen key. Replace them if they show excessive wear. The last thing you want is to be descending a mountain without braking ability!

A dirty chain can make you expend more energy to cover the same distance. It can also wear down the teeth of your chain rings and freewheel cogs. The simplest way to clean a dirty chain is to use an old toothbrush and a commercial solvent. (Never use gasoline as a solvent!) This can be done with the chain on the bicycle, or you can remove it. Either way, work carefully. If you don't remove the chain, advance it by turning the cranks. When you have finished applying the solvent to the chain and its contact points, wipe everything down with a clean cloth. Then apply fresh lubricant sparingly. Excessive lubricant only collects more grit and grime.

Given the rough treatment that mountain bikes sometimes endure, it's a good idea to check the bolts that hold the cranks to the chain rings. Tighten them if they are loose. Also, inspect the headset (the handlebar assembly). Use a headset tool to tighten the nuts if necessary.

*A weekly inspection will help you avoid serious breakdowns.*
*Here a rider makes a minor adjustment to the brakes.*

Wheel spokes are more than decorative. They are a structural part of the wheel, and periodically they come loose or break. Faulty spokes can warp a wheel and cause it to wobble.

Tighten loose spokes with a spoke wrench and replace broken or missing spokes.

A weekly check may sound time consuming, but it needn't be. Most of the items mentioned can be inspected visually, or with a jiggle here and a thump there. Besides, a weekly inspection is more efficient than a breakdown on the road when you're miles from anywhere!

*Courteous behavior to others sharing the trail
will help ensure open space for mountain-bike users.*

# ECOLOGY AND ETHICS

A recent *San Diego Union-Tribune* article bemoaned the fact that "reckless bicyclists have endangered public safety and threatened delicate wildlife habitats." Every year, the complaints against mountain-bike riders increase, as have reports of trails that have been banned to them. The future of mountain biking is ours to enjoy, or lose—and you can make a difference.

Put yourself in the shoes of the hiker, horseback rider, or naturalist sharing the trail with you. Always yield them the right of way. Be respectful of an area's serenity— a primary reason why people escape to the backcountry—and try not to disrupt that peace with loud or rowdy behavior.

Riders everywhere can help to create a positive image about the sport of mountain biking. All it takes is a simple code of conduct.

# CODE OF CONDUCT

- Try to avoid skidding. A skid uproots vegetation and increases the chances of erosion.

- Never ride in a restricted area. Observe posted signs.

- Save high-speed riding for organized races.

- Stay on marked trails and paths. Straying from already existing trails destroys vegetation and causes additional erosion.

- Carry your bike over fragile, soft ground.

- Stop and dismount your bicycle when a horse is coming toward you on a trail. Stand to the side of the trail between your bicycle and the horse. If you are approaching a horse and rider from behind, ask for permission to pass. When it is given, pass only in a wide area.

- Yield to hikers; and when passing, do so at a slow pace. Be friendly and courteous, and they won't object to sharing the trail with you and other mountain bikers.

- Leave the trail clean and litter-free for the next rider, hiker, or horseback rider to enjoy.

- Join a mountain-bike group and donate a day every month to work with local land-management bureaus on trail maintenance. If there isn't a group, start one. The International Mountain Bicycling Association can tell you how.

*High-speed riding is best left to organized events.*

*Serious mountain bikers donate their time and energy*
*to preserving existing trails and preparing new ones.*

Conflict with other trail users is avoidable. Your courtesy, thoughtful riding, and constructive action will win over opponents and preserve trails for future mountain-biking enthusiasts.

Happy trails!

# ORGANIZATIONS AND PUBLICATIONS

You may want to know more about organized racing events, festivals, and tours. The following organizations and publications may be of help.

## ASSOCIATIONS

International Mountain Bicycling Association
P.O. Box 7578
Boulder, CO 80306

National Off-Road Bicycle Association (NORBA)
1750 East Boulder Street
Colorado Springs, CO 80909

Backcountry Bicycle Tours
P.O. Box 4029
Bozeman, MT 59772

Coyote Adventure Company
P.O. Box 267
Nevada City, CA 95959

Slickrock Adventures
P.O. Box 1400
Moab, UT 84532

Vermont Mountain Bike Tours
P.O. Box 526
Pittsfield, VT 05672

Whistler Backroads Mountain Bike Adventures
P.O. Box 643
Whistler, British Columbia V0N 1B0
Canada

# BOOKS

Abramowski, Dwain. *Mountain Bikes.* New York: Franklin Watts, 1990.

Allen, Bob. *Mountain Biking.* Minneapolis: Lerner Publications, 1992.

Coombs, Charles. *All-Terrain Bicycling.* New York: Henry Holt, 1987.

Olsen, John. *Mountain Biking*. Harrisburg, PA: Stackpole Books, 1989.

van der Plas, Robert. *Mountain Bike Handbook*. New York: Sterling Publishing Co., 1991.

Woodward, Bob. *Sports Illustrated Mountain Biking: The Complete Guide*. New York: Sports Illustrated Winner's Circle Books, 1991.

## MAGAZINES

*Mountain Bike*
33 East Minor Street
Emmaus, PA 18098

*Mountain Bike Action*
P.O. Box 958
Valencia, CA 91380

*Mountain Biking*
7950 Deering Avenue
Canoga Park, CA 91304

*Outside*
P.O. Box 54729
Boulder, CO 80322

# INDEX

*Numbers in italics refer to illustrations*

# ABOUT THE AUTHOR

Larry Dane Brimner has written many books for Franklin Watts, including *Voices from the Camps: Internment of Japanese Americans During World War II*. Among the First Book titles that he has authored are *Rock Climbing, Rolling. . . In–Line,* and *Karate*. When he isn't writing, Mr. Brimner visits elementary schools throughout the country to discuss the writing process with young authors and readers.